PRAYING WITH
THE JEWISH TRADITION

Praying with
THE JEWISH
TRADITION

Compiled by

Elias Kopciowski

Translated by

Paula Clifford

Introduction by

Lionel Blue

William B. Eerdmans Publishing Company
Grand Rapids, Michigan / Cambridge, U.K.

Selection © 1983 Figlie di San Paolo, Rome, as *Ascolte Israele.*
Translation and Introduction © 1988 The Society for Promoting
Christian Knowledge

This edition © 1997 Wm. B. Eerdmans Publishing Co.
255 Jefferson Ave. S.E., Grand Rapids, Michigan 49503

Printed in the United States of America

02 01 00 99 98 97   7 6 5 4 3 2 1

Library of Congress Cataloging-in-Publication Data

Praying with the Jewish tradition / compiled by
Elias Kopciowski ; translated by Paula Clifford ;
introduction by Lionel Blue.
p.   cm.
ISBN 0-8028-4317-4 (pbk. : alk. paper)
1. Judaism — Prayer-books and devotions —
English.   I. Kopciowski, Elias.
BM665.K65   1997
296.4′5 — dc21   97-7871
CIP
r97

Scripture quotations marked (NIV) are from the HOLY
BIBLE: NEW INTERNATIONAL VERSION. Copyright
© 1973, 1978, 1984 by the International Bible Society. Used
by permission of Zondervan Bible Publishers.

CONTENTS

INTRODUCTION

Christians used to refer to Jews as 'the people of the book', and there was no doubt about which book it was — though it wasn't a book in fact, but a library. They referred to the Hebrew (and Aramaic) Scriptures which are the common inheritance of both faiths, which each had developed differently.

But the Old Testament (or Tenach, to use the Jewish term) is not the best book for understanding the religion of modern Jews because it has a limitation which it shares with all scriptures. Its text is closed, though it remains of course open to commentary. Indeed, Jewish literature takes the form of commentaries upon commentaries upon commentaries on it, each enfolding the interpretations of a previous generation. The text of the Talmud, too, is closed. It came to an abrupt halt in Babylon in the sixth century of the common era. And so, too, is the Zohar, the text of the Jewish mystics. Only through their commentaries can they grow.

But the Jewish prayer book is different. Unlike other holy books, it is still open-ended and unfinished. It can still absorb the faith, the longings, the triumphs and the failures of this generation and the generations that will succeed it, as it found room for all those that went before it.

It includes blocks of biblical faith that cluster round the affirmation of God's unity in Exodus.

These are followed by rabbinic petitions, philosophical statements, medieval hymns, psalms, and modern prayers trying to assimilate and interpret the holocaust and the rise of Israel. The collection is too alive to be consistent. Each layer of faith lives alongside the others — they do not cancel each other out. Consistency is found in cemeteries; the untidiness of growth is the quality of life.

Jews have a long history — four thousand years of it — double the Christian length. During that time they have worshipped at mounds of stones, desert altars and movable arks, in two solid static temples, in synagogues, and in shtiebels. Patriarchs, priests, scribes, rabbis, rebbes, seers, mystics, and ordinary folk have been leading their little worship communities in prayer. Each phase has left its mark and its message in the liturgy. If a Christian therefore wishes to understand his fellow Jews, he should attend their prayers and give his attention to the holy book which is the best known among them — their prayer book.

Why should he or she do so? There are many reasons. First, there has been a subtle but definite change in Christian-Jewish relations since the end of the last war, for reasons which we do not completely comprehend — the horror of the holocaust perhaps, or the Holy Spirit. But the medieval cold war seems to have died down, and a real desire to understand each other has replaced it.

For a Christian there is also another reason. Both Jesus and his early disciples lived in the world of early rabbinic Judaism, when the modern prayer book took its present form. They prayed its prayers, in the synagogues of their time. They could not know the liturgy of the Church which would proceed from them but were familiar with the forms of worship still used by Jews today. Christianity therefore, for its own self-understanding, needs to know those forms. Otherwise Jesus is torn away from his historical and human background, and is limited to an icon.

But those are contemporary, communal reasons. There is another, even more important — the enrichment of the prayer life of the individual reader.

Jewish prayers are built out of much of the same material as Christian prayers. They, too, are a mosaic of quotations from the Psalms and the Scriptures which both share. But they are built up into different patterns, and it is this mixture of familiarity and difference which makes them disconcerting and enriching.

Jewish prayers take the form of blessings. They ask little and are God-centred. God is like this or that, they say (or both), and the world which he fashioned is so, and this is the way a wise and good man should journey through it. The prayers frequently come in pairs. If one is optimistic, its fellow points out the vanity of human aspiration. If one is concerned with God's destiny for Jews, its fellow corrects this particularism with prophecies which include all human beings and indeed all creation. A worshipper walks, so to speak, between the different emphases of faith. He will use his own life experience to guide him through the divine dialectic of daily life.

Such prayers are important in an age when spirituality is easily confused with sentimentalism, and feeling with faith. In these prayers our experience of God is subordinated to his experience of us. He is the objective fact, not we. As the rabbis put it — he is the place of the universe, though the universe is not his place.

It is not easy to translate prayers. I say this out of experience, having edited and translated with Rabbi Dr Magonet the liturgy for the Reform Synagogues in Great Britain. Hebrew is concise where English is diffuse, and it uses a terse, concrete vocabulary. God is father, judge, physician and friend — but he is not your pal!

I approached the translations in this book with interest, but with some scepticism — a new translation of well-worn material! My doubts died away as I read them. They gave the real sense of the original — more discursive, it is true, because a word-for-word replacement is not possible, but still a translation, not a paraphrase.

This book will be used no doubt in study courses and libraries. But it will be most useful where the reader prays and worships. Its spirituality complements, but does not contradict, a Christian's experience of God, and he or she has the assurance that in some form these prayers were used by Jesus and those who knew him. Even if they seem strange now, they were not strange to the holy family or the apostles.

The destiny of Jewish prayers has been various. Take the simple blessings, over bread and wine, which still mark the Sabbath and the festivals and are said in every Jewish home. In Christian worship they have become the centre of the sacrament of the Eucharist. This book will help its readers to experience the richness which has flowed from the early revelations to our forefathers, and the continuing revelation which leads all generations, including our own, to love the Lord, and express this love in prayer.

Lionel Blue

PRAYERS OF PRAISE AND THANKSGIVING

O Lord, open my lips,
and my mouth will declare your praise.

Psalm 51.15 NIV

Priestly blessing

The Lord bless you
and keep you.
The Lord make his light
shine upon you.
The Lord turn his face towards you
and give you peace.

Numbers 6.24-26

Hear our cry

O Lord, hear our cry
and have mercy on us.
Receive our prayer
and have pity on us.
Accept our supplication
and have compassion on us.
Almighty God,
Father of great and infinite love,
never have we prayed to you
in vain.

From the 'supplications' recited on weekdays
after the Amidah. *Probably medieval*

While the earth was without form

O Lord, ruler of the world,
even while the earth was without form
you were King.
And you will still reign
when all things are brought to an end.
You are supreme
and will never be equalled.
You are power and might:
there is neither beginning nor end
in you.

Authorship uncertain.
Probably 10th-11th century AD

Hallelujah!

Praise, O servants of the Lord,
praise his blessed name
now and for evermore.
From the rising of the sun
to the place where it sets,
the name of the Lord
is to be praised.
The Lord is exalted
above all peoples and nations.
God's glory
is above the heavens.
Who is like him
who sits enthroned on high,
who stoops to look down on us?
His throne is in heaven
yet he looks at us on earth.
He raises the poor from the dust;
he lifts the needy from the ashheap
and gives them their rightful place
among the princes of this world.
Through his grace
he gives children
to the woman who once was barren;
now she rejoices with her many sons.
Praise, O praise the Lord, hallelujah!

Psalm 113. One of the Hallel *psalms**

* *Hallel* is the group of psalms (Psalms 113–118) sung in the
synagogue on certain festivals.

6

O Lord!

O Lord, the Creator
of all the world,
all living things
bless you!

If . . .

If my lips could sing as many songs
as there are waves in the sea:
if my tongue could sing as many hymns
as there are ocean billows:
if my mouth
filled the whole firmament with praise:
if my face
shone like the sun and moon together:
if my hands
were to hover in the sky like powerful eagles
and my feet
ran across mountains as swiftly as the deer;
all that would not be enough
to pay you fitting tribute,
O Lord my God.

*Hymn probably composed in the
Talmudic period, 3rd-5th century AD*

My trust is in you

I hear you speak and I praise you:
my trust is in you.
I ask for nothing
and need no explanation:
can a clay vessel ask the potter
'What have you done?'
I sought you and found you
and you are
a tower of strength,
a shelter,
a stronghold and a refuge.
Your light
is a special light
that can never be veiled nor dimmed.
Fire and water
and stars moving through the heavens
all bear witness to your great power
and your glory.
You created
the universe and its harmony.
By your power alone
creation is sustained:
you never grow weary.
Who could ever describe your glory,
you whose word alone created the world?
You established your holy dwelling
in the highest heavens,
yet you also set a seat next to Moses
in the tent of the Congregation.
You sent prophecies and signs.
You showed yourself in light,

without form,
for your divinity cannot be bounded.
There is no limit to the deeds
that testify to your supreme wisdom,
nor can they ever be numbered.
Oh, how blessed are they
who fall down before you in silent worship.

*Jehudah Ha-Levi**

---

* *Jehudah Ha-Levi* was born at Toledo, Castille, in 1080 and probably died while on a pilgrimage to the Holy Land in 1140. He is regarded as the greatest Jewish poet since King David and is the author of the famous philosophical work *The King of the Kazars*.

Hymn to the Creator

The earth is full of your goodness,
your greatness and understanding,
your wisdom and harmony.
How wonderful
are the lights that you created.
You formed them
with love, knowledge and understanding.
You endowed them
with strength and power,
and they shine very wonderfully on the world,
magnificent in their splendour.
They arise in radiance
and go down in joy.
Reverently
they fulfil your divine will.
They are tributes to your name
as they exalt your sovereign rule
in song.

Hymn probably composed in one of the
groups of mystics that sprang up at the
time of the Second Temple

My strength and stay

You, my God,
are eternal and all powerful:
through you and in your time
the dew comes down,
the wind blows
and the rain falls.
You feed the living.
You uphold those who waver,
those torn apart by doubt,
those in anguish
and those, indeed, who risk falling into sin.
You restore the sick
and set the prisoners free;
you bring the dead back to life
according to the promise that you gave
to those who lie in darkness
in the earth.

One of the nineteen Benedictions
that make up the Amidah*

---

* The nineteen Benedictions of the *Amidah* are recited aloud
three times a day while standing to face east, i.e., towards the
city of Jerusalem.

Who is there like you?

Every living soul
shall bless your name,
O God.
All created things
will give you glory and thanksgiving.
Eternally
you are God,
and no one can stand before you.
Who but you
offers freedom and help,
nourishes and redeems us,
sustains and saves us,
and at all times
views with unfailing compassion
our sorrow and distress?
There is no one
but you.

Hymn probably written in the
Talmudic period, 3rd-5th century AD

Holy, holy, holy

Like the choir
of holy seraphim
seated about your throne
we sing:
Holy, holy, holy is the Lord Almighty:
may the whole earth
shine with his glory!

*Fragment composed by mystics at the
time of the Mishnah, based on Isaiah 6.
Included in the public recitation of the* Amidah

14

MEDITATIVE PRAYERS

Who is like you, O Lord —
majestic in holiness
and awesome in glory,
working wonders?

Song of Moses —
Exodus 15.11 NIV

15

We, the living

The Lord
remembers us and blesses Israel.
He blesses those
who love and fear him,
small and great alike.
O my God, bless, prosper and increase
our family.
May we be blessed by the Lord,
the Maker of heaven and earth.
Behold, his kingdom is in the highest heavens
and the earth he has given to us, the descendants
   of Adam.
It is not the dead who praise the Lord
nor those who go down to eternal silence.
It is we, the living,
who praise the Lord.
We who live
bless his holy name for evermore.

Based on Psalm 115.12-18

Pilgrims' song

Lift your eyes to the hills.
Where will your help come from?
It will come from the Lord,
the Maker of heaven and earth.
May he uphold you
and not let your foot slip.
May he be your defender
and watch over you
as he watches over Israel.
The Lord protects you,
he is your shade at your right hand.
Do not be afraid:
the sun will not harm you by day
nor the moon by night.
May the Lord
keep your soul from all harm.
May he watch over your coming and going
now and for evermore.

From Psalm 121

They hurry out

The beloved sons of Zion
pray for one another;
they awake from sleep
to follow the ways of the Almighty.
Already they call upon the Lord from their beds
and hurry out when it is barely light . . .
The way is long!

Part of a selicah* *attributed to Benjamin,*
son of Abraham of the Anavim, who lived
in Rome in the 13th century

* The *Selicah* is a particular form of prayer seeking divine forgiveness.

The soul you gave me

The soul you gave me is pure,
my Lord:
you gave it life
and you preserve it within me,
and at the end, when the time comes,
you will take it away,
only to give it back to me one day.
But as long as that soul is in me
it will worship you,
O Lord my God,
the God of my fathers,
from whom one day
the dead will receive back their souls.

Thanksgiving recited on waking in the
morning. From the Babylonian Talmud, Ber. 60b

Think!

Think, O mortal man,
think very carefully:
what are you?
where do you come from?
who in the beginning gave you life?
who gave your heart and mind
both strength and intelligence?
So waken your slumbering spirit
and stand in wonder:
God is good!
But beware!
The most hidden things
are from God alone;
while man's mind
is incapable of understanding them
and of pondering their cause.
He can do no more than cry aloud:
May God be praised!
May he be exalted and adored!

Jehudah Ha-Levi

He inclines his ear

How my heart rejoices
to know that the Lord hears me
and that he inclines his merciful ear
to my call!
All my life
I have not ceased to call upon his name;
and when death holds out his hands to me,
when mortal anguish, trouble and pain
torment my heart,
then too I will call upon his name.
O Lord, my Lord,
save my soul.
O God of holiness and compassion,
grant me once more
your great mercy!

From Psalm 116.1-5

He watches over us

O Israel,
trust in the Lord your God.
He is your help and shield.
You who fear him, trust in the Lord,
for it is he who watches over us!

From Psalm 115.9, 11

At nightfall

Blessed are you, O Lord our God,
King of the universe!
At your word night falls.
In your wisdom
you open heaven's gates,
you control the elements and rotate the seasons.
You set the stars in the vault of heaven.
You created night and day.
You cause the light to fade when darkness comes
and the darkness to melt away
in the light of the new day.
O ever-living and eternal God,
you will always watch over us
your creatures.
Blessed are you, O Lord,
at whose word night falls.

Attested in the Talmud, Ber. 11b

24

I commit to you . . .

O Lord my God,
who sets my soul free,
you are my rock,
my refuge when fate is against me,
and my shelter;
as I fall asleep
I commit to you my spirit and my soul,
and as I awake
I commit my body and spirit
into your holy hands
for your protection.
And I have nothing to fear.

Prayer based on biblical verses
and recited before sleeping

In the palm of your hand

In the palm of your hand
you hold our souls
which we entrust to you:
the souls of the living
and the souls of the dead.
In the palm of your hand
you lovingly hold
the divine spirit
of all things living.
To you, O Lord,
O God of truth,
I commit now the spirit that is within me.
Heavenly Father,
your name alone is holy,
you are unchanging
and your kingdom is eternal;
you will reign over us for ever.

Compiled from biblical verses and recited
at evening prayers after the Shema.*
Included since post-talmudic times

* The *Shema* is the main part of the daily liturgy, recited morning and evening. The *Shema* is above all the solemn proclama-
tion of the unity and uniqueness of God, entailing the duty to
love him and obey his commandments and to instruct children
in the holy doctrine, so that it may be handed down for ever.
The *Shema* consists of three prayers from the *Torah* (Deuteronomy 6.4-9, 11.13-21 and Numbers 15.37-41).

Look down on us, O God

Look down from the gates of heaven,
O Lord,
on those who fall before you
and kneel in your presence,
addressing their pitiful prayer to you.
Look down on the faint-hearted
whose strength has left them.
Hear and receive their prayer
as an offering
or a sacrifice.

By an unknown medieval author.
Early version of a selicah

We trust in you

O Lord our God
and God of our fathers,
we trust in you
for our lives
which we commit into your holy hands,
for the soul dwelling within us
which you preserve,
and for the wonders
that you perform daily in the world
from morning to night.
Eternally holy God,
whose mercy is constantly renewed,
our hope is ever in you;
you have never betrayed us
or abandoned us,
nor hid yourself from us.

From the Amidah

Saviour

You will bear up the wretched
in your powerful hands.
You save the poor,
the needy and the oppressed
from the anger of violent men.

Hymn probably composed in talmudic
times, 3rd-5th century AD

In my anguish

In my anguish
I cried out to my God.

If the Lord is with me
can I ever fear man?
How much better it is
to trust in the Lord
than to trust in man!
To take refuge in the name of the Lord
than to trust in princes.
And even when I am greatly oppressed
I trust in you, O God,
and my persecutors
shall all be struck down.

When they swarm around me
like frantic bees
they will be destroyed
like burning thorns.
You are my strength
and my song, O Lord!
And see, from the tents of the righteous
there goes up a shout of joy
that God's right hand
does mighty things:
God's right hand is all-powerful!
I shall not die
but will yet live
to tell of God's greatness.

Even though God may punish me
he will not allow me to die.
Arise, open wide
the golden gates of righteousness
to enter and pay homage
to the Lord my God!
This is the great and holy gate
through which only the righteous may enter.

We give glory to you, O Lord,
because you have heard us
and saved us.
Your works
have won us salvation
which is a marvellous and beautiful thing
in the eyes of men.
The stone that was rejected
and thrown aside
has become the cornerstone
of your building.

This is the day of rejoicing
that the Lord has made.
Let us rejoice and be glad in it!

From Psalm 118

In your mercy

In your mercy, O my God,
save me from the proud,
and help me not to be proud myself.
Deliver me from sin
and keep my tongue from doing wrong
by committing slander, speaking evil
and quarrelling
with anyone at all.
Blessed are you, O God,
who have guided us and made us a holy people
through your precepts
and who commanded us
to study your law.

Text quoted in the Talmud, Ber. 16b

Be at rest

Be at rest,
O my soul, and do not be fearful,
for the Lord has been good to you;
he has saved you from death
and granted you life.
My God
delivers my eyes
from bitter tears
and guides my steps
to keep me from falling into the abyss.
And if it is your will, O Lord,
I shall yet live
in a way that is pleasing to my God
in the land of the living.

From Psalm 116.7-9

Hear our cry

O Lord our God,
the God of our fathers!
Hear our cry
and do not refuse our supplication,
for we know that we have sinned
and have fallen short.
We have strayed
from your commands
and from your holy laws.
What can we say to you,
most high God?
You who dwell in the heavens,
what can we tell you?
Do you not know
our deepest and most secret thoughts?
You know the secrets of the universe
and the deeply hidden thoughts of men.
You see into our hearts and souls
and nothing can escape you.
Forgive us, O Lord,
all our sins
and pardon our misdeeds!

*From the 'supplications' recited
after the* Amidah *on weekdays*

What can we say?

What can we say in our defence,
O God?
What can we confess to you
who reign on high
and know all mysteries and all revealed things?
You know
all that is hidden deep within the universe
and the most secret thoughts of men.
You know
the true feelings of every heart.
You, my Lord, are a righteous judge,
O God of our fathers!
May it please you now, O Lord,
to forgive us all our faults,
our failings and our sins.

*From the 'supplications' recited
after the* Amidah *on weekdays*

PRAYERS FOR MERCY AND BLESSING

May our cry be heard in heaven and find mercy!

Morning prayers

You are my God

I will be betrothed to you for ever, O Lord,
and my bonds shall be bonds
of justice and equity,
goodness and mercy.
I will be betrothed to you
in complete faithfulness
because you are my God.

*Based on Hosea 2.19-20**

---

* These verses from the prophet Hosea are recited while the leather strap of the *tephillah* for the arm is passed round the middle finger, symbolising union with God.

Before falling asleep

O Lord, grant that this night
we may sleep in peace.
And that in the morning
our awakening may also be in peace.
May our daytime
be cloaked in your peace.
Protect us and inspire us
to think and act only out of love.
Keep far from us all evil;
may our paths be free from all obstacles
from when we go out
until the time we return home.

Babylonian Talmud; Ber. 55b, 9b

Mercy

Have mercy, O God,
on all who are sorrowful,
those who weep and those in exile.
Have pity on the persecuted and the homeless
who are without hope;
those who are scattered
in remote corners of this world;
those who are in prison
and ruled by tyrants.
Have mercy on them
as is written in your holy law,
where your compassion
is exalted!

Be with me

You are my refuge,
my fortress and my defence.
Be with me today
and keep me from dying
and from every misfortune.
Grant that now and always
I may find grace and pity
in your sight
and in the sight of those
whom I may meet along my way.

From the Talmud, Ber. 60,2

Bless us, O Lord!

Bless us, O Lord,
in this coming year.
May dew and rain
be a source of blessing.
Bless to our use the fruits of the earth
and let the earth rejoice in them.
And bless all that we do
and the work of our hands.

From the Amidah

Stretch out your hand

O Lord, I pray
that you will inspire my heart
to do what is worthy of you.
Do not let me fall into sin.
Do not allow my lower instincts
to prevail.
Stretch out your hand
and lead me into the ways of righteousness
and of your holy laws.
Put temptation far from me.
Make my stubborn heart
humble and obedient,
that I might return to you
along the path that you desire;
so that it may come to pass
for me and my sons as
you promised, and as is written:
'the Lord will turn your heart
and the hearts of your sons
to perfect love,
to the Lord your God,
and then you will enjoy
true life.'

Talmud 60b

The presence of God

Let our eyes see your return to Zion
and to Jerusalem, which was once your city.
Blessed are you, O Lord our God,
who will restore
your holy presence to Zion.

From the Amidah

Gather in your people

O Lord,
sound your mighty trumpet
to gather in your dispersed people,
to bring them running
at its great and terrible call.
Come, come, O Israel,
from the four corners of the earth,
back to Israel.
Bring your people back
to their homeland,
the land that we long for unceasingly . . .
Blessed are you, O Lord,
who gather in
your dispersed people Israel.

From the Amidah

May your kingdom come

May the greatness and holiness of our God
be acknowledged
throughout the world that he created
of his own free will!
O God,
grant that your kingdom may come this day
while we yet live.
Let this be brought to pass. Amen.

May your ineffable name
be praised, blessed and exalted,
although it is far above all human speech and
    blessing,
far above all words that come from human lips.
Let this be brought to pass. Amen.

May there be mercy and peace and a life of
    serenity
in Israel and for all who have given time and
    energy
to studying God's law,
who have followed the way of the teachers
with infinite love, joy and devotion.
Let this be brought to pass. Amen!

*Composed at the time of the Second Temple**

* The prayer 'May your kingdom come', composed at the time
of the Second Temple, was recited by the Master, or orator, at
the end of study. But since it is so full of faith and hope the
custom arose of reciting it in times of crisis and oppression,
until finally it became customary to recite it during periods of
mourning to stress the acceptance of God's will.

Blessing on the community

O God who blessed our fathers,
Abraham, Isaac and Jacob,
bless us all and bless all Israel.
Bless us, I pray,
fathers, mothers and sons and their loved ones.
Bless those who dedicate places of prayer,
those who pray and those who act generously;
those who give hospitality to strangers,
help the poor,
and devote themselves to the well-being of the
community.
Holy and blessed God,
who protect and reward your people,
give them and our brothers in Israel
salvation and forgiveness of their sins,
grant them blessing and peace
and keep evil far from them.
Amen.

PRAYERS FOR THE STUDY AND OBSERVANCE OF THE LAW

Blessed is the Lord, the King of the universe, who is our guide!

Hear, O Israel . . .

Hear, O Israel,*
the Lord our God,
the Lord is One.
Love the Lord your God
with all your heart and with all your soul
and with all your strength.
These commandments that I give you today
are to lie upon your hearts.
Impress them on your children:
talk about them when you sit at home
and when you walk along the road,
when you lie down and when you get up.
Tie them as symbols
on your hands, that they may do good,
and on your foreheads,
that your eyes may see and have mercy.
Write them on the doorframes of your houses
and on the gates of the city,
as a reminder that it is the dwelling place
of the Eternal God.

Deuteronomy 6.4-9
(This translation based on NIV)

---

* 'Hear, O Israel . . .' is a three-part prayer recited twice a day:
on getting up in the morning and before going to bed at night.
See p. 26.

Good and evil

You gave us, O God,
understanding, reason and intellect.
O my Lord,
grant that we may use them
to discern good from evil
and to do good.

From the Amidah

Give me the strength . . .

O Lord,
keep my lips from speaking evil, untruth
    and deceit.
Give me the strength not to react
against anyone who insults me.
Let it be my delight to keep your commandments
and help me to a full understanding of your laws.
Let me not be proud.
May the wicked plans of those who seek to harm
    me
be brought to nothing.
Grant me wisdom, patience and understanding,
mercy and compassion,
and give me the means to live.
O God, who established the harmony of creation,
give peace to mankind
and to Israel.

Mar ben Rabina.
Closing meditation of the
Amidah; *Talmud, Ber. 17a*

Eternal love

You gave your people Israel
eternal love;
you taught us laws and ordinances,
statutes and institutions.
Inspire us, O God,
inspire our hearts with love
to meditate on the statutes of your will,
so that our study of your holy law
may always be joyful
and undertaken with gladness.
The law is the purpose and object
of our existence.
Let us meditate on it day and night
and never deprive ourselves
of your love!

Talmud, Ber. 11b

Gladden our hearts

Grant us blessings, O Lord,
through your holy feasts,
that we may know living joy
and peace in our hearts.
As once you blessed us,
so bless us again now and always.
Make Israel holy by your ordinances
and turn our minds again
to your holy law.
Fill us with your goodness
and gladden our souls with your salvation.
Make our hearts pure
as we serve you in love and truth.
Let us greet with joy and gratitude
the feasts dedicated to you.

Attested in the Palestinian Talmud, Ber. 9,3
and in the Babylonian Talmud, Ber. 49a

SABBATH PRAYERS

Remember the Sabbath day
*by keeping it holy**

Exodus 20.8 NIV

* The *Sabbath* is the supremely holy day, established at Creation, as is stressed in the fourth commandment: 'Remember the Sabbath day by keeping it holy. Six days you shall labour and do all your work, but the seventh day is a Sabbath to the Lord your God. On it you shall not do any work, neither you, nor your son or daughter, nor your manservant or maidservant, nor your animals, nor the alien within your gates. For in six days the Lord made the heavens and the earth, the sea, and all that is in them, but he rested on the seventh day. Therefore the

Lord blessed the Sabbath day and made it holy' (Exodus 20.8-11 NIV).

The orthodox Jew does not work on the Sabbath because on the seventh day the Lord himself ceased his work of creation.

In the peaceful and harmonious atmosphere of the home as the Sabbath begins the mother lights two candles and recites the blessing: 'Blessed are you, O Lord our God, King of all the world, who made us holy with your ordinances and commanded us to kindle the Sabbath lights.'

The lighting of the candles (or of an oil lamp with seven spouts, one for each day of the week) means that the Sabbath is beginning and that all work has come to a halt. The Sabbath light (like that on festivals) symbolises the light shining in the home on the holy day of the Lord. The lighting of it, which is the special responsibility of the mother, emphasises the woman's fundamental importance in the family: it is she who lights the fire in the hearth and who is the source of light that in a special way on the holy day of the Lord gives her family peace and joy.

The *menorah* is the seven-branched candlestick that was placed in the Tabernacle during the wanderings in the desert; then, when it was built, in the Temple at Jerusalem (see Exodus 25.31-40). The three arms on each side of the *menorah* are turned towards the central light and symbolise the six working days turned towards the most important day, the Sabbath. This is to signify that even on the days mainly given over to secular activity there is the obligation to remember the paramount importance of spiritual values which find their most complete and elevated expression on the Sabbath, the holy day of the Lord.

Ner tamid is the 'perpetual light' that is kept lit before the holy Ark, symbolising our absolute duty to see that God's word never grows dim in our hearts and minds, and as a constant reminder that divine teaching should illumine our whole lives and guide all our actions. In the Tabernacle and in the temple of Jerusalem the purest olive oil had to be used for *Ner Tamid*, being specially prepared for the purpose.

Meeting the Sabbath

The Sabbath is at hand,
let us go up with joy to meet it!
It is the source of joy and blessing.
It was the last day of creation
and also the first day,
since it brought to completion
God's great work of creation.

O holy city of King David,
O Jerusalem,
awake now,
for your time of weeping is ended!
Arise, shake off the dust
that still covers you.
Come up out of the sad ruins
in which you lie.

O my people,
put on your ceremonial garments once more,
for God will have mercy
and the Messiah who will come from Bethlehem
will be among us to redeem our souls!
O awake, awake!
Come forth,
your light is here!
Shine forth and repeat your song:
divine light already shines upon you!

Why do you still tremble?
Why is your face
covered in dark shame and dishonour?

See, all the wretched will find refuge in you
and out of the ruins
there will arise to new life
a city more beautiful and more holy than before!
Those who wreak terror and destruction in you
will be punished
and your God will find joy in you,
just as the bridegroom rejoices at the sight of the
        bride.
You will look out in all directions
and you will love and serve your God
with great gladness,
for his Messiah has come among us
and in him we shall all find our joy and happiness.

Come, O Sabbath,
O worthy crown of the people!
Come into the midst of the faithful,
O precious gem!

Solomon Alcabez Ha-Levi,
Kabbalist, Safed 1500-1570.
Hymn recited at the
beginning of the Sabbath

Sabbath blessing before the meal

Blessed are you, O Lord our God,
King of the universe,
who created the fruits of the vine.
Blessed are you, O Lord,
who made us holy with your ordinances
and in your love gave us the Sabbath day
in remembrance of your creation.
It is the most important of all our holy days,
recalling the exodus from slavery in Egypt,
because you chose us out of all the peoples
and in your love gave us the gift
of this holy day.
Blessed are you, O Lord, who made
        the Sabbath holy.

Blessing on the wine

Blessed are you, O Lord our God,
King of the universe,
who made this bread come forth from the earth.

Blessing on the bread

Blessing after the meal

Help us, O Lord,
to obey all your commandments
and to observe the seventh day,
the great and holy Sabbath:
for this is the special day
which was consecrated of old to you.
This is the day when we stop work
in acknowledgement of the rest
which you have been pleased to give us.
Let neither sorrow nor pain
cast a shadow over this day of rest.
Now let the consolation of Zion
come quickly in our lifetime;
and even though
we have eaten and drunk our fill
let us not forget
the destruction of your holy dwelling.
So, O God, in your mercy
do not forget us or reject our pleas,
for you are great and holy,
O Lord our God.

Additional passage for the Sabbath

O Lord . . .

O Lord, when you gave us your decrees
you commanded us to observe the Sabbath
in remembrance of the seventh day of your
      creation:
we heard and were obedient.
And it is for us
a perpetual memory,
the inheritance of those who are pure and faithful.

When you decreed it to be the most holy day,
Israel made it a day of joy and love;
you set free this people of yours
and gave them this sacred day
as a solemn and everlasting sign of the Covenant
between you and your people;
this is the day we remember and observe.

In six days
you created the whole world,
but on the seventh
you ceased your work and gave your people
      and all Israel
a day of peace and rest.
It is to honour your holiness
on this Sabbath day
that we lift to you
our praises, our psalms and our prayers.

When you gave your holy laws,
Moses and all the people
sang a song of joy and gladness, crying out:

'Who will be like you, my Lord!
Who can be like you, surrounded in glory!
You are worthy of great praise,
you who accomplish wonderful things,
and your holiness
is of unsurpassing greatness.'

The people were astonished and wondered
at your miracles,
as when at the Red Sea
you opened up a way for your defenceless people,
and they worshipped you, crying:
'Our God will reign for ever!'
So salvation comes quickly
to those who on the day of rest, your day,
being overwhelmed with joy and gladness
obey the commandment of the day of rest!

And once again, Lord,
set your people free,
that they may no longer
be subject to persecution and oppression!

*From the blessing which, in some rites,
is pronounced after the* Shema *at evening
prayers at the beginning of the Sabbath*

The day of rest

When your great work of creation was complete,
on the seventh day
you sat down on your glorious throne.
Surrounded by joy
and peace and glory
you named this day of rest
the Sabbath,
the day of love and gladness
and of prayer.

At the close of the Sabbath

May the week that is just beginning*
be happy and joyful.
May Elijah the prophet come quickly among us
with the Messiah of the line of David.
For the Jews
this has been a day of gladness and jubilation.
With joy we have celebrated
the Sabbath here at home.
May God always come to our aid
and grant us success in our work.
May God bless us
and give us sons.
May he give us prosperity and plenty
and make us holy!
May he be near us
and guide our steps in his great goodness.

* A special plaited candle with several wicks is lit and the prayer
for the end of the Sabbath is said before the new week begins,
in a ceremony called *Havdalah* (separation). The importance
of this is stressed in the Talmud, Ber. 33.

PRAYERS FOR THE PILGRIM FEASTS

Bless us, O Lord,
*through your holy feasts.**

* The pilgrim feasts are: *Pesach, Shavuot* and *Sukkot.* They are
the times when the people of Israel would make their pilgrimage
to Jerusalem. The three festivals are linked by the fact that they

all commemorate the flight of the Jews from Egypt and their sojourn in the desert.

Pesach commemorates the actual Exodus and the signs and miracles that accompanied it.

Shavuot is the day when God gave Moses the Ten Commandments on Mount Sinai.

Sukkot commemorates the tents set up in the desert in the forty years that the Jews dwelt there before entering the Promised Land.

Each festival also has an agricultural significance: *Pesach* is the spring festival, *Shavuot* the summer one and *Sukkot* the autumn festival. Since the Israelites were essentially an agricultural people, the cycle of the seasons and their crops were very important. When coming to the Temple at Jerusalem, pilgrims would bring with them an offering of first fruits on the day of *Shavuot*.

Remember

O Lord our God and God of our fathers,
look mercifully on us and our forefathers
and your city Jerusalem;
remember the Messiah,
of the line of your servant David,
and do not forget your people Israel;
grant us on this holy day
mercy and compassion,
blessing and peace,
for we look to you,
O God of love, mercy and compassion.

*From the Talmud, Ber. 29b and
from the Sopherim Tractate 19,11*

Let those who want come and eat

This bread that we eat*
is the bread of affliction
that our fathers once ate
in the land of Egypt.
Whoever is hungry
let him come and rest,
whoever is in need,
let him come among us
and celebrate the Passover.
This year we are still here in exile,
but next year we shall be free in Israel!

* Before reciting the text 'Let those who want come and eat' a
basket is raised containing, among other things, three loaves of
unleavened bread.

This evening is different!

Why is this evening
different from all other evenings?
Because we were once slaves
of the Pharaoh in Egypt;
but the Lord heard our voice:
he felt our sorrow
and understood our oppression;
with his powerful hand
and his outstretched arm
he led us out of Egypt.
Then we were at last set free.
Blessed is the Lord,
who promised salvation to Israel:
he has kept his promise
and kept the Covenant he established
      with Abraham.

Passover

When the temple
was still standing firm and secure
in our city Jerusalem
our fathers used the sacrifice of the paschal lamb*
as a reminder that God
spared the homes of the Israelites
and passed over them,
to punish only the Egyptian oppressors.
And our fathers bowed down before the Lord.

* The text is recited while those at table are shown the lamb's
shankbone.

Matzah

The unleavened bread*
that we eat this evening
reminds us of the day our fathers left Egypt:
there was no time to lose
so they baked bread on hot stones in the desert
without leavening it.

* Those at table are shown a loaf of unleavened bread.

Maror

These bitter herbs*
will always remind us of the harsh oppression,
the misery of slavery
and the labour
to which our fathers were condemned
in the land of Egypt.

* Those at table are shown bitter herbs taken out of the basket.

Always

In every age
we relive history
as if we ourselves were still in slavery
and felt the breath
of the divine Spirit helping and saving us
and leading us by the hand
into the land promised to our forefathers.
And with hearts filled with gratitude and delight
we celebrate and praise
him who has set us and our fathers
  free from slavery
and who has saved us from our oppressors.
It is he who changes sorrow into joy,
mourning into rejoicing
and darkness into light.

When we came out of Egypt

When Israel came out of Egypt;
when Jacob left the people who had enslaved him;
Judah became God's sanctuary
and Israel his dominion.
Then the sea looked and fled,
and the Jordan turned back.
Even the mountains shook,
and the hills trembled like frightened lambs.
Why was it, O sea, that you fled?
Why, O Jordan, did you turn back?
And you, mountains and hills,
why did you shake and tremble?
At the presence of the Lord
the whole earth trembles and shakes.
At the presence of the Lord,
the God of Jacob,
who turned the rock into a pool
and changed the hard rock
into springs of water.

Psalm 114

For the Feast of Weeks

I will always remember
the wonderful deeds of the Lord
when Israel was in Sinai,
when Moses led the people out of Egypt
into freedom.
They stood purified at the foot of the mountain
to receive your law, your holy law;
which they swore to obey for ever.
And Israel was a holy nation
in the midst of all the nations,
a holy thing and precious to the Lord.

High on the mountain your voice, Lord,
        was heard,
revealing great things:
and then the blind saw your light
and the deaf heard your voice,
while the dumb opened their mouths
        to speak of you.

And then, O Lord, you revealed yourself
to those who had sought you
and you said to them:
I am the rock,
I am your shield and your defence,
I am the only God.

You appeared in majesty, glory and splendour
to deliver your commandments.
And young and old alike

were surrounded by the same glory that
        surrounds you
and by your greatness.
And still today
in my heart and soul and in my every thought
I bless the marvels and wonders
that you, O Lord, perform.

For the Feast of Weeks (Shavuot).
Medieval composition by an
unknown author

For the Feast of Tabernacles

Who would not worship you, O Lord God,
O King most high?
Surrounded in glory you revealed yourself to us
and offered us the crown of your holy law.

You guided our fathers in the desert;
you spread out a cloud above their heads
to shelter them from the burning sun by day
and you kindled a glowing flame
to light their way by night.
You protected the tents that they set up
as their homes in the desert;
and so you demonstrated again
your great love for your people.
You inclined to them
and came down on to the mountain
surrounded in glory,
to light the Ark with your words.

You who created the world
with your powerful hand,
who lifted up your sons
and crowned them with your holy laws
and ordered them to set up tents in the desert,
raise up, I pray,
the house of David our King,
that they may return to dwell in the midst of the
    people Israel.
Then the Righteous One, God's Messiah,
will come to bring salvation
and to guard the holy city.

For the Feast of Tabernacles (Sukkot). *Medieval*

Rejoicing in the Law

My soul is thirsty for God.
My heart and body will sing to the Lord!
With my whole being
I will lift up a song to the living God
who alone is God.
God in his great wisdom, goodness and power
created all that has being
and all that remains hidden from mortal eyes.
He is exalted in the heights of heaven
yet all created things
reflect and mirror his great and all-powerful
     Majesty.
But what is man beside you,
almighty and omnipotent God?
He is dust and mire;
the instincts of his heart
lead him to do evil;
as he is flesh
he turns to wicked deeds.
He must repent and seek forgiveness
before he dies.
O Lord, teach Israel your laws and statutes,
that are the full fount of life.
Blessed be you, O Lord, who hold
the essence of all living things in your hands!
Remember, I pray, the love of our fathers
and forgive us their children!

For the Festival of Simhat Torah*
*('Rejoicing in the Law'). Abraham ibn Ezra***

* *Simhat Torah* is the festival of the *Torah,* the day when the synagogue was completed and the reading of the *Sepher Torah,* the Torah scroll, was resumed. This is handwritten with the utmost care on parchment, by someone highly qualified who sets about his task in a state of special purity. Today the scrolls of the law are kept in the Holy Ark *(Aron ha-kodesh)* in the synagogue.

** *Abraham ibn Ezra,* philosopher, poet and biblical commentator, was born at Toledo in 1090 and died around 1170.

For the Feast of Lights

These candles
which now we light
are in remembrance of the miracle of our
    deliverance,
of the wondrous and glorious deeds
that you performed for our fathers of old
and still perform for us today
through your holy priests.
For the eight days of Hanukkah
these candles are holy,
and we cannot look at them
without giving praise and honour to you, O Lord,
for the wonders and miracles that you have
    performed
and for your glory.

For Hanukkah.* *Hymn at the lighting
of the candles. Talmud, Sopherim 20,6*

* *Hanukkah* is the feast of lights and of freedom. It commemorates the successful rebellion led by the Maccabees (or
more precisely Asmonides) against Antiochus IV Epiphanes,
King of Syria (who also ruled Palestine), who wanted to impose
idol worship on the Jews. During the struggle to be free of

Antiochus' tyranny those fighting for freedom and their faith reconquered Jerusalem and found the Temple desecrated. After they had rededicated it, they had for *Ner Tamid* (see p. 58) just one small bottle of oil, closed with the High Priest's seal, which was barely enough for one day. Miraculously the oil lasted for eight days, the time needed to prepare more. To celebrate this miracle the *Hanukkah* candlestick is kept alight every year during the festival of *Hanukkah*.

Hanukkah is a nine-branched candlestick with eight lights corresponding to the eight days of *Hanukkah* and a ninth light called *shammash*.

We give you thanks, O God

We give you thanks, O God,
for your mighty acts and victories;
for the conflicts and the deliverance
that you won for us in days of old
and still do today.

We remember, O God,
the day when Mattathias and his sons
rose up in rebellion
to be free of the tyranny of the Greeks
who forbade observance of your law and
      commandments,
and condemned acting in accordance with your
      will
as you made it known to us.

In your great holiness
you upheld them and saved them.

You delivered the strong into the hands of the
      weak,
and the many into the hands of a few.

You delivered sinners into the hands of the sinless
and gave the wicked into the hands of the
      righteous;
the proud you placed in the hands of those
who had dedicated their lives to studying your
      holy law.

And all this that the world might know
the greatness and holiness of your name.

Included in the Amidah *and in the
blessing after the meal during the
eight days of* Hanukkah

New Year

The gates of mercy are about to open;
as the sun sets I lift up my hands
in reverence and worship,
in prayer to God
at this solemn moment of divine judgement.
You who dwell in the heights of heaven,
remember the promise
that you made of old to Abraham,
and save your people
who are lost and oppressed;
give ear to those who blow the *shophar;*
hear their prayers
and tell Zion that the day of salvation is at hand
and that soon the Messiah will come!

For Rosh Ha-Shanah *(New Year)**

---

* *Rosh Ha-Shanah* (New Year) commemorates the day when
the world was created. During the day the *shophar* or ram's
horn is blown several times, to commemorate the faith of
Abraham, who was prepared to sacrifice his son Isaac, the child
of his old age, in obedience to God's will. With this test of
Abraham's complete obedience thus accomplished God ordered
him not to harm the boy, thereby totally forbidding human
sacrifice. A ram was sacrificed in place of Isaac (see Genesis 22).

PRAYERS OF REPENTANCE ON THE DAY OF ATONEMENT

Be pleased, O Lord, to look with compassion on us sinners!*

---

* Throughout the day of *Kippur* (The Day of Atonement), which, like all Jewish holy days, begins at sunset, the Jews keep a solemn fast, abstaining from all forms of food and drink. But even more important than the fast is the mind and spirit in which the Jew approaches this day of penitence and expiation. Several times during the day a confession is read together which lists practically every sin, including the most serious, because the whole community is also responsible for the sin of the individual, in that, if they had intervened with moral or material help at the right time, the sinner would probably have been saved in time.

The true fast

This is God's message:
'Peace to all men,
to those far and near,
and I will heal them.
But the wicked are many,
they are like the tossing sea
that rages and cannot rest,
whose waves cast up mud and mire.
There is no peace for the wicked!'

He says:
'You seek me, my people;
yet on the day of your fasting
you spend your time in quarrelling and strife,
in law-suits and selfishness!
No, you cannot fast
and expect your voice to be heard in heaven!
Is this the fast in which I delight?

The fast I want from you is quite different!
Break the chains of your wicked passions
and loose the fetters of tyranny and oppression
that the oppressed may be set free.
Shatter every yoke once and for all!
Share your bread with the hungry;
open your doors to the homeless;
give clothing to those whom you meet
    along the way.
Do not turn away from your own flesh and
    blood!
Then your light will break forth like the dawn

bringing healing to your soul.
Then righteousness will go before you;
the glory of God will mark your way.
Then you will call upon your God
and he will answer you:
you will cry to him for help
and he will turn to you and say:
"Here am I!" '

Haftoroth* *for the Day of Atonement.*
Based on Isaiah 57 and 58

---

* The *Haftoroth* consists of extracts from the prophets and is
read after the Torah on the Sabbath and on other occasions.

You hold out your hand

You reach out your hand to sinners
when they return to the narrow way
and hold out your right hand
to greet those who are penitent:
O Lord God, you have taught us
to confess all our sins;
accept our humble repentance.
May it be an acceptable sacrifice to you
according to the promise you have given us!

Prayer recited at the end of Kippur.
Included in the Talmud, Ioma 87b

God of compassion

The Lord is merciful and compassionate;
he is the true God!
He pours out his goodness on the descendants of
　　the just.
He forgives wickedness
and pardons the sin of those who turn their
　　hearts to him.
Forgive us, O Lord!
Bear with us!
Our sin and wickedness are great.
But you, O Lord, are forbearing
and supremely full of compassion
towards those who seek your forgiveness.
You are always ready
to grant mercy and pardon
and are therefore even more
to be worshipped and adored.

Based on Exodus 34.6ff.

Father, forgive

Our Father,
forgive all our misdeeds
and wipe away our sin,
for you are great and compassionate;
your mercy knows no bounds.

God of grace

O God, our King,
your throne is surrounded in glory and grace:
your rule is mercy;
you pardon your people when they fall into sin
and grant mercy to sinners;
you graciously stoop to hear all human creatures;
I beg you, Lord, do not deal with mankind
according to the evil they have done!

You alone!

Cancel out, I pray,
all our transgressions,
for it is you
who forgives Israel.
Without you
we would have no pardon or forgiveness.
You alone are our hope!

Included in the Amidah *for Kippur.*
Based on the Talmud

Hear us!

O my God!
You who have pity on the poor,
hear us!
You who pity the oppressed,
hear us!
You who have pity on anguished hearts,
hear us!
You who had pity on our father Abraham
when he was on the mountain of Moriah,
hear us!
You who had pity on our father Isaac
when he was laid on the sacrificial altar,
hear us!
You are the God of compassion,
who listens to the prayers of the righteous,
the God-fearing and the pure:
hear us and grant our requests!
O merciful Lord, save us!
O God of compassion, redeem us!
O God of pity, have mercy on us I pray,
and on those whom we love.
Make your light shine out of the darkness
to light our way,
for the love of your great and holy name.

From various 'supplications' in the Mishnah

Before the close of day

O Lord, when you see all that we have done,*
our sins and our misdeeds,
I beg you have mercy
before the close of the day!
You are resplendent on high
in a mantle of light;
when you mete out punishment
hear our cry
before the sun goes down!

The wretched come to you,
great and lowly alike,
in fear and hope;
in your mercy grant them forgiveness
before the close of the day!
Then open the door to your people
who turn to you in penitence.
Let us be changed
before the sun goes down!

Pour out on us your cleansing power
and accept our ransom and our prayers
before the close of the day!
Grant us long life
and forgive us our sins
before the sun goes down!

* The text is derived from an acrostic and interspersed with
biblical extracts, possibly dating from the 7th or 8th century.

Come, eat!

Come, eat your bread with joy!
Drink your wine with peace in your heart.
Your fast has been pleasing to the Lord!

On the final day of Kippur. *The words are accompanied by the blowing of the* shophar.

PRAYERS FOR DAILY LIVING

Blessed be he who enters in the
name of the Lord!

Hallel Psalm 118.26

Seven blessings for a wedding

Blessed are you, O Lord our God,
King of all the world
and creator of the fruit of life.

Blessed are you, O Lord,
who created all things for your glory.

Blessed are you, O Lord,
who created man in a day.

Blessed are you, O Lord,
who created man in your likeness
and established him
that he might increase and multiply.
As a woman rejoices and is glad
when she gathers her children into her family,
so blessed be the Lord,
who rejoices when his sons
are gathered in and return to Zion.
Let all who are present rejoice
and remember the joy that was heard
on the day of creation.
Blessed be the Lord,
who gives joy to the bridegroom and bride!

Blessed be the Lord,
who has granted to the bride and bridegroom
jubilation and song,
joy and contentment,
love and peace,
friendship and fellowship.

Straightway their cries of joy shall ring out
to the Lord and to Jerusalem the holy city.

May the voices of the bridegroom and the bride
resound in jubilation
and may the hearts of those who witness their joy
be glad.

Blessed be the Lord,
who gladdens the bridegroom with the bride.

On the birth of a baby boy

May peace be upon us,
upon our homes
and upon our land, Israel.
Behold our joy
that a new baby boy has come into our midst!
May the Messiah come in his lifetime!
May he prosper in the shadow of the Lord!
May he find peace and shelter in following the
      ways of the Lord!
May he understand his holy laws
and may the divine light of the voice of God
be all around him!

*Short hymn recited at the beginning
of evening prayers on the Sabbath if a
baby boy has been born during the week*

On the birth of a baby girl

Bless, O Lord, this baby girl
as you blessed our mothers in the past!
May your blessing be upon her as she grows up:
may she grow in peace and health
and in perfect serenity.
May her father and mother rejoice at her marriage.
May the future bring her sons,
as well as riches and honour.
May her sons be blessed with vitality
and be for her a source of happiness
even in her old age!

From a prayer recited at the naming
of a baby girl

Blessing after meals (1)

Blessed are you, O Lord our God
and king of all,
who in your love
sustain the world with goodness and compassion
and in your mercy
provide food for all creatures.
You in your infinite mercy
will stay with us and will fulfil the needs of all
your creatures,
of all those formed on the day of creation.
In your grace
stretch out your hands in blessing
and all your creatures will be satisfied.
Blessed are you, O Lord,
who in your mercy
sustain the living!

This thanksgiving is traditionally
attributed to Abraham.

Blessing after meals (2)

You who gave our fathers for all time
a special land that was rich and fertile,
you who gave us the covenant of circumcision
and gave us the law,
our life and our food;
we give you thanks.

Blessing after meals (3)

Have mercy on us, O Lord,
and on your people Israel
and your city Jerusalem!
Have mercy on Zion
where your great glory shines,
on the kingdom of David, your anointed one,
and on your holy and glorious temple
where once we called upon your name.
O Lord, you feed us,
provide for our needs
and make us happy:
keep us free from all misfortune!
Do not let any distress
force us to seek refuge in human generosity:
make us dependent on you alone
and on your good and abundant providence.
Let us not remain in ignorance in this world!
Let us not be unworthy of the blessedness
of the world to come,
for we trust in your holy and powerful name.
May there come swiftly in our lifetime
the prophet Elijah
and the Messiah, the Son of David,
to bring us at last
joyful news from the furthest places.
While we partake joyfully of food and drink
let us not forget
that our holy temple, which is your dwelling,
lies in ruins.

Blessing after meals (4)

O Lord,
rebuild Jerusalem soon
in our lifetime,
that we may rejoice to see at last
the restoration of your holy city
as it once was.

Guest's blessing after meals

Most holy God,
bless the table at which we gather today.
Keep it well supplied with all food and drink.
May this table flourish and be a source of blessing
like that of our father Abraham.
Let the hungry come
and find food and comfort.
May the Lord bless
the father of this home and his family.
Hear his prayers in this world
and make him worthy
and deserving of blessedness in the world to come.
May his fortunes prosper,
may he never be struck by adversity;
may there never be any occasion for him
    to do evil
both now and in the future.

Before a journey

O Lord our God
and God of our fathers!
Mercifully direct and guide our steps
to our destination,
and let us arrive there
in health, joy and peace!
Keep us from snares and dangers,
and protect us from any enemies
that we might meet along the way.
Bless and protect our journey!
Let us win favour in your eyes
and in the sight of those around us.
Blessed are you, O Lord,
who hear and grant our prayers!

Before sleep

Give us rest and peace, O Lord our God.
Let us still be alive
when the sun rises tomorrow.
Spread over us your mantle of peace
and your protection.
Inspire in our hearts thoughts of goodness.
Save us, O God,
for your mercy's sake.
Protect us from our enemies
and keep far from us
evil and conflict,
hunger and affliction.
Keep us from stumbling
and falling into danger.
Shelter us in the shadow of your wings,
for you are our protection and salvation;
goodness and mercy are yours.
Watch over our going out and coming in.
Spread over us your mantle of peace.
Blessed are you, O Lord, who offer protection
    and peace
to your people Israel
and to your holy city
Jerusalem.

Blessing recited on the evening of the Sabbath
and of festivals, after the Shema

For the sick

Send down your angel
who in his mercy gives comfort and relief
to those who suffer.
Let the sick and infirm be healed.
Lighten and relieve their pain.
Let them have respite from their suffering
that they may see your light.
Let healing come swiftly with the dawn.
Blessed are you, O Lord,
who uphold the sick on their bed of sorrow!
May their days once more be good
and their years happy!
Blessed are you
who uphold, save and restore the sick.

A prayer of the dying

May God be with me
and with his messenger whom he has sent to
    greet me
and lead me to heaven.
May the Lord who is great and blessed
look upon me,
have pity on me and grant me peace.
May he give me greater strength and courage
that I may not be fearful or afraid.
For the angels of God are about me
and God is with me wherever I may be.
O God, be present with me and grant me rest.
Set my soul free from the prison of my body
and it will praise your name
when it receives its just reward
    among the righteous.
Do not be sad, O my soul,
do not be troubled but take hope,
for your salvation comes from God.
O God of compassion and mercy,
soon I will find expiation for my sins
that I may be pure in your presence.
Awake now, O winds!
Blow from the north and from the south!
Blow along the paths of paradise
that I may feel its fragrance
and enjoy its more glittering fruits.

PRAYERS OF HOPE FOR THE MESSIANIC AGE

The gates of glory are about to open!

Hope

O Lord our God,
inspire in us love and respect
for your wonderful works.
Let every created being turn to you;
may they all act in harmony,
with hearts unimpaired,
that your will may finally be fulfilled.
For the earth is yours,
you are all-powerful,
you give strength and love to all that you created.
O Lord, give honour to your people
and glory to all those who fear you.
Give hope to those who come to you in love.
May all who trust in you be free to speak.
May Israel and your city Jerusalem have joy.
Let the power of your servant David flourish
      once more;
may his light come now
and shine on our days.
And then the righteous will see and be glad.
Honest hearts will rejoice
and the virtuous will exult.
Then hatred will vanish from the earth.
All godlessness will disappear like smoke
because you will drive out evil from the world.

*Thought to date from the first
drafting of the Talmud*

The day of the Messiah (1)

May the time draw near
when there will be neither night nor day!
Help us, O God, to understand
that the day is yours
and the night is yours also.
Place guards in your holy city
to stay there both day and night.
Make the darkness of night
shine in the brilliant light
of your day.

Traditional song concluding the
Passover order (Seder)

The day of the Messiah (2)

How beautiful on the mountains
are the banners of the herald
who comes proclaiming peace!
He brings joyful news
that salvation is at hand
and says to Zion:
Your God reigns!
Rejoice, then, O sons of Zion
and of Jerusalem:
behold the King; the Messiah comes!
He is righteous and victorious
yet in humility he rides on an ass's foal.
The Lord says:
See! I send you a messenger
to prepare the way for me!
And immediately,
after so much wandering, so much seeking,
there will appear to you the shining vision
of the Lord in his Temple:
it is the Angel of the Covenant,
the Lord of hosts!
He says to you,
Behold, before the great and terrible day
    of the Lord
I will send you again
the prophet Elijah;
he reconciles the hearts of fathers to their sons
and the hearts of sons to their fathers,
that my coming shall not be one of sorrow
    but of joy.
The days are coming, says the almighty Lord,

when the shoot of David will be among you,
and then he who is the true King
will reign with great wisdom,
righteousness and compassion.
See, in those days
Judah will be saved
and Israel will live.

Recited during afternoon
prayers on the Sabbath.
Based on a compilation from Isaiah

Hasten . . .

Hasten, O Lord,
the coming of the Messiah,
the shoot of your servant David.
Through your salvation
his kingdom will be restored
and peace will flourish.
O God of heaven,
grant us your salvation!

From the Amidah